MICHAEL JACKSON

WISE PUBLICATIONS
PART OF THE MUSIC SALES GROUP
LONDON / NEW YORK / PARIS / SYDNEY / COPENHAGEN / BERLIN / MADRID / TOKYO

ALSO AVAILABLE IN THE *REALLY EASY PIANO* SERIES...

ABBA
25 GREAT HITS. ORDER NO. AM980430

CHART HITS
21 BIG CHART HITS. ORDER NO. AM993377

CHILDREN'S FAVOURITES
20 POPULAR HITS. ORDER NO. AM998745

CHRISTMAS
24 FESTIVE CHART HITS. ORDER NO. AM980496

CLASSICAL
36 POPULAR PIECES. ORDER NO. AM980419

CLASSICAL FAVOURITES
24 WELL-KNOWN FAVOURITES. ORDER NO. AM993366

COLDPLAY
20 SONGS FROM COLDPLAY. ORDER NO. AM989593

ELTON JOHN
24 CLASSIC SONGS. ORDER NO. AM987844

FRANK SINATRA
21 CLASSIC SONGS. ORDER NO. AM987833

GREAT FILM SONGS
22 BIG FILM HITS. ORDER NO. AM993344

GREAT SHOWSTOPPERS
20 POPULAR STAGE SONGS. ORDER NO. AM993355

JAZZ
24 JAZZ CLASSICS. ORDER NO. AM982773

LOVE SONGS
22 CLASSIC LOVE SONGS. ORDER NO. AM989582

NEW CHART HITS
19 BIG CHART HITS. ORDER NO. AM996523

NO. 1 HITS
22 POPULAR CLASSICS. ORDER NO. AM993388

POP HITS
22 GREAT SONGS. ORDER NO. AM980408

SHOWSTOPPERS
24 STAGE HITS. ORDER NO. AM982784

TV HITS
25 POPULAR HITS. ORDER NO. AM985435

60s HITS
25 CLASSIC HITS. ORDER NO. AM985402

70s HITS
25 CLASSIC SONGS. ORDER NO. AM985413

80s HITS
25 POPULAR HITS. ORDER NO. AM985424

90s HITS
24 POPULAR HITS. ORDER NO. AM987811

21st CENTURY HITS
24 POPULAR HITS. ORDER NO. AM987822

50 FANTASTIC SONGS
FROM POP SONGS TO CLASSICAL THEMES. ORDER NO. AM997744

50 GREAT SONGS
FROM POP SONGS TO CLASSICAL THEMES. ORDER NO. AM995643

50 POPULAR SONGS
FROM POP SONGS TO CLASSICAL THEMES. ORDER NO. AM994400

PIANO TUTOR
FROM FIRST STEPS TO PLAYING IN A WIDE
RANGE OF STYLES — FAST! ORDER NO. AM996303

ALL TITLES CONTAIN BACKGROUND NOTES FOR EACH SONG PLUS
PLAYING TIPS AND HINTS.

PUBLISHED BY
WISE PUBLICATIONS
14-15 BERNERS STREET, LONDON, W1T 3LJ, UK.

EXCLUSIVE DISTRIBUTORS:
MUSIC SALES LIMITED
DISTRIBUTION CENTRE, NEWMARKET ROAD, BURY ST EDMUNDS,
SUFFOLK, IP33 3YB, UK.
MUSIC SALES PTY LIMITED
20 RESOLUTION DRIVE, CARINGBAH, NSW 2229, AUSTRALIA.

ORDER NO. AM1000604
ISBN 978-1-84938-552-7
THIS BOOK © COPYRIGHT 2010 BY WISE PUBLICATIONS,
A DIVISION OF MUSIC SALES LIMITED.

MUSIC ARRANGED BY BARRIE CARSON TURNER.
MUSIC PROCESSED BY PAUL EWERS MUSIC DESIGN.
EDITED BY OLIVER MILLER.
PRINTED IN THE EU.

YOUR GUARANTEE OF QUALITY
AS PUBLISHERS, WE STRIVE TO PRODUCE EVERY BOOK TO THE HIGHEST
COMMERCIAL STANDARDS. THE MUSIC HAS BEEN FRESHLY ENGRAVED AND
THE BOOK HAS BEEN CAREFULLY DESIGNED TO MINIMISE AWKWARD PAGE
TURNS AND TO MAKE PLAYING FROM IT A REAL PLEASURE.
PARTICULAR CARE HAS BEEN GIVEN TO SPECIFYING ACID-FREE, NEUTRAL-
SIZED PAPER MADE FROM PULPS WHICH HAVE NOT BEEN ELEMENTAL
CHLORINE BLEACHED. THIS PULP IS FROM FARMED SUSTAINABLE FORESTS
AND WAS PRODUCED WITH SPECIAL REGARD FOR THE ENVIRONMENT.
THROUGHOUT, THE PRINTING AND BINDING HAVE BEEN PLANNED TO
ENSURE A STURDY, ATTRACTIVE PUBLICATION WHICH SHOULD GIVE YEARS
OF ENJOYMENT. IF YOUR COPY FAILS TO MEET OUR HIGH STANDARDS,
PLEASE INFORM US AND WE WILL GLADLY REPLACE IT.

WWW.MUSICSALES.COM

Blame It On The Boogie

Words & Music by Elmar Krohn, Thomas Meyer, Hans Kampschroer, Michael Jackson Clark & David Jackson Rich

The 1978 release by The Jacksons of their version of this disco hit prompted what the press called 'The Battle of the Boogie' as it was a rare occasion when two artists charted at the same time with the same song. More unusually, they had very similar names, although the other, composer Mick Jackson, was no relation.

Hints & Tips: On the second page, the rhythm should be secure and articulated; play an accent on each of the first three left-hand chords in each bar to bring out the syncopation. The semiquavers at the end of each bar (from bar 9 onwards) should be exciting – experiment with a staccato touch on some of them. To reflect the excitement in the words from bar 17, a crescendo throughout this eight bar section would work well.

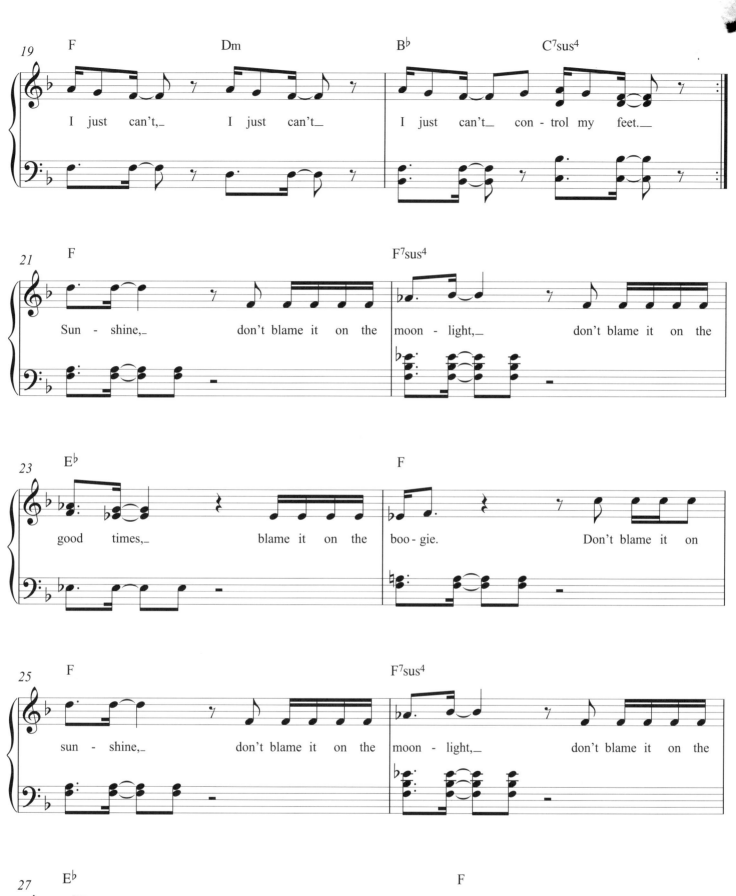

Ain't No Sunshine

Words & Music by Bill Withers

This song was a breakthrough hit for Bill Withers and won the Grammy for Best R&B Song in 1972. Michael Jackson's version was the third single taken from his debut solo Motown album *Got To Be There*, which Rolling Stone magazine described as 'slick, artful and every bit as good as the regular Jackson 5 product'.

Hints & Tips: Make sure that the rhythm of the first two notes doesn't become lazy. It should be snappy and energetic, and the left-hand response in the following bar should be strong and articulated. From bar 17, try a crescendo towards bar 19, with another crescendo from bar 20–22, to help make the melody more effective and add interest. On the last line, try to make the repeat of 'anytime she goes away' slightly quieter, like an echo.

Slow rock-blues feel ♩ = 80

Ain't no sun-shine when she's gone. It's not warm when she's a-

-way. Ain't no sun-shine when she's gone,__ and she's al-ways gone too

long an-y-time she goes a-way. Won-der this time where she's

gone, won-der if she's gone to stay. Ain't no sun-shine when she's

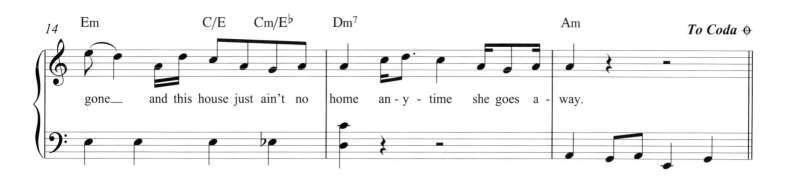

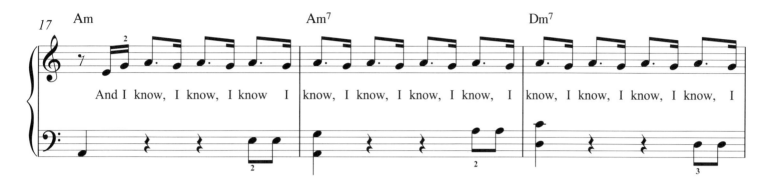

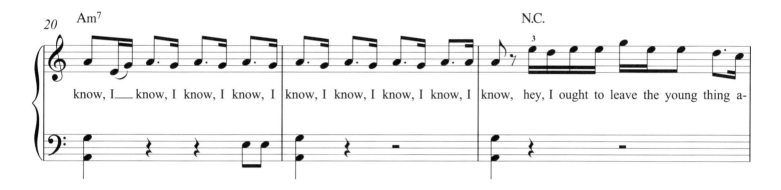

Baby Be Mine

Words & Music by Rod Temperton

In making his record-breaking 1982 album *Thriller*, Michael Jackson was inspired to create an album where each song was strong and a potential single. This joyful number though, with its vintage soul sound typical of the early 1980s, was one of only two of the nine tracks not to be released as a single.

Hints & Tips: Due to the frequent syncopation from the start it is helpful to count out a bar or two silently before beginning, to give yourself a strong foundation on which to put these complicated rhythms. When possible, bring out the left hand (for example at bar 3 and at bar 7) as it often has interesting answering melodies and moves the harmony in different directions.

9

Burn This Disco Out

Words & Music by Rod Temperton

This was the closing track on *Off the Wall*, Michael Jackson's fifth studio album, an amalgam of funk, disco-pop, soul, soft rock, jazz and pop ballads, from which he became the first solo artist to have four singles from the same album reach the Top 10 of the Billboard Hot 100.

Hints & Tips: Be careful in bar 14 not to stretch the $\frac{2}{4}$ bar; make sure the rhythm is accurate. From bar 19–22 a crescendo would work well, and although the left hand is rhythmically quite interesting throughout this song, make sure that you provide a strong and secure accompaniment with the chords.

Can You Feel It

Words & Music by Michael Jackson & Jackie Jackson

Written by Michael Jackson and his brother Jackie, this song with a message provided a pulsating opening track to *Triumph*, The Jacksons' album released in 1980. Lead vocals were shared by Michael and younger brother Randy, who had recently triumphed over extreme injuries sustained in a near fatal car accident.

Hints & Tips: This song has a very characteristic bassline which is heard first in bar 1 and happens no fewer than 11 more times, so feel free to bring this out in between the vocal lines.

Cry

Words & Music by R. Kelly

From Michael Jackson's 2001 album *Invincible*, a collection of entirely new material, this anthemic song talks about all of the problems in the world, covering such issues as war, loneliness, lying, depression, suicide, miracles and faith, suggesting that, if everyone pulls together as one, we can make the world a better place.

Hints & Tips: One of the main features of this song is syncopation, which will only be effective if a clear pulse has been set in the first few bars, so pay particular attention to the bassline. Keep the tempo flowing!

Girlfriend

Words & Music by Paul McCartney

Originally recorded by Paul McCartney and his band Wings and released on their 1978 album *London Town*, McCartney mentioned this song to Michael Jackson at a Hollywood party as one that he might like to record, though Quincy Jones was unaware of this when he too suggested it for the 1979 album *Off the Wall*.

Hints & Tips: The left hand is almost as important as the right hand in this piece, providing an important link in between each vocal line. Take care to play this accurately, particularly at the end of bar 22 where it gives a strong upbeat before the vocal line returns. In the final eight bars especially, the accompaniment should be strong and supportive, and a diminuendo might work well in the last bar.

Human Nature

Words & Music by Steve Porcaro & John Bettis

Producer Quincy Jones selected this song for Jackson's album *Thriller* after hearing a cassette of demos given to him by David Paich of the rock band Toto. This track, by Toto keyboard player Steve Porcaro, caught his attention. Subsequently it has become a firm favourite among Michael Jackson fans.

Hints & Tips: Be careful at bars 3 and 11 that the crisp rhythm on 'city' and 'walls won't' is accurate and energetic. In the final chorus from bar 17 a crescendo would work nicely, building a little more on each repetition of 'why, why'. Then to balance this and to round of the piece effectively, the final 'I'm like loving this way' could be slightly quieter and the song could slow down slightly in the last bar.

The Lady In My Life

Words & Music by Rod Temperton

This soulful ballad is one of three included on *Thriller*, an album which successfully used music videos as promotional tools and confirmed Michael Jackson as one of the pre-eminent pop stars of the late 20th century, enabling him to break down racial barriers by his appearances on MTV and with the US President.

Hints & Tips: The accompaniment in this song should be rich and supportive throughout. Make sure that the bass note 'G' is sustained strongly from bar 1 to bar 2. This may mean that you have to play the chord above it slightly quieter to help the sound carry. The melody becomes quite tricky from bar 13 onwards, so be sure to work out all the fingering carefully. Above all this song should have a laid-back feel and careful practise will help this.

Man In The Mirror

Words & Music by Glen Ballard & Siedah Garrett

Released in 1988, featuring the Andrae Crouch Gospel Choir, this uplifting song about making a change and realizing that it has to start with you became the fourth of five consecutive No. 1 hits for Michael Jackson from his album *Bad* and following his death attained the highest position of his 16 entries in the UK top 75.

Hints & Tips: From bar 17, the mood changes with the introduction of the A minor chord, so it could become quieter here. When it returns to the major key at bar 22, the brighter mood could gradually return, with crisper rhythms and stronger accompaniment.

the wind is blow-ing my mind.___ I see the kids in the street___ with not e-

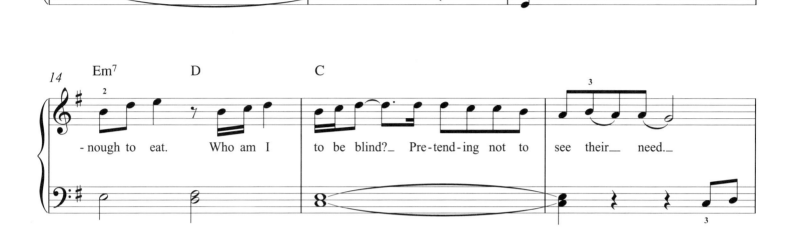

-nough to eat. Who am I to be blind?___ Pre-tend-ing not to see their___ need.___

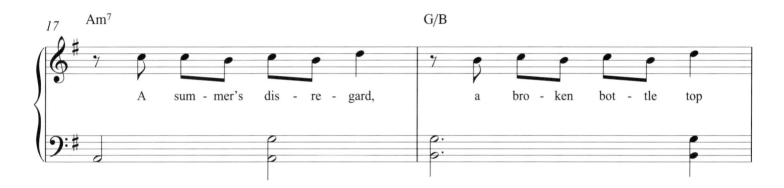

A sum-mer's dis - re - gard, a bro-ken bot - tle top

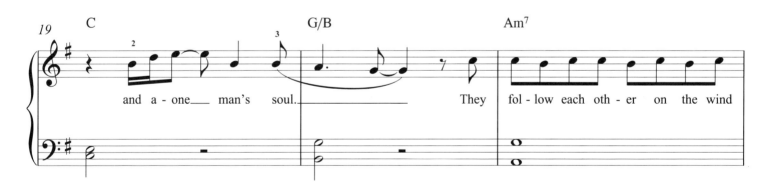

and a-one___ man's soul.___ They fol - low each oth - er on the wind

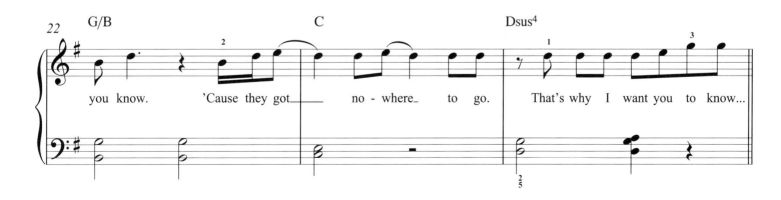

you know. 'Cause they got___ no - where___ to go. That's why I want you to know...

Off The Wall

Words & Music by Rod Temperton

Released in 1980, this underrated and relatively obscure Michael Jackson song about getting over troubles, with its trademark soaring chorus, became the third Top 10 single from the album of the same name and eventually one of four, something only achieved before from a single disc studio album by Fleetwood Mac.

Hints & Tips: The left hand in this piece should be strong and driven throughout and in the small sections where it plays alone it must be decisive and rhythmic. You might like to experiment with different dynamics for each repetition on the first page. Enjoy the instrumental section from bar 23, and make sure every note is exciting.

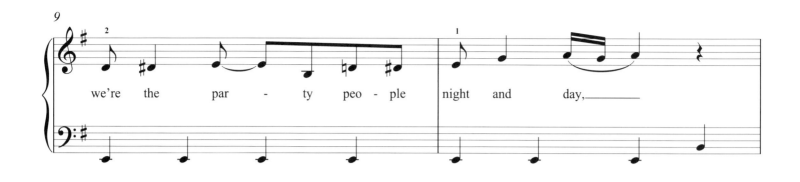

we're the par - ty peo - ple night and day,_____

liv - in' cra - zy, that's the on - ly way._____ So,_____ to -

- night,_____ got - ta leave that nine - to - five____ up - on the shelf,_

_____ and just en - joy your - selves. Groove,_____ and let the

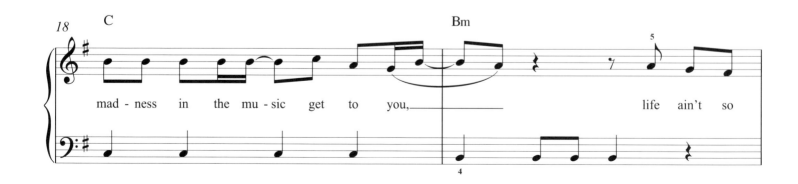

mad - ness in the mu - sic get to you,_____ life ain't so

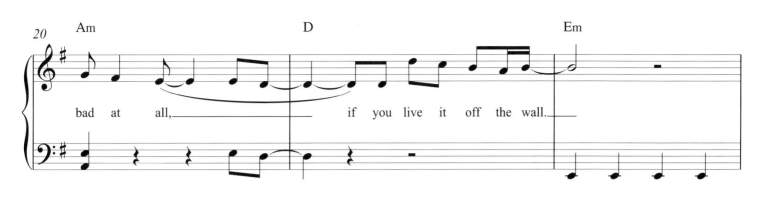

bad at all,_____ if you live it off the wall.____

To Coda ⊕

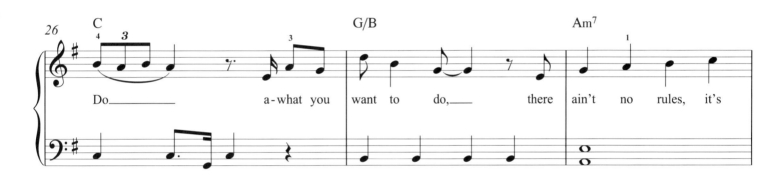

Do_____ a-what you want to do,____ there ain't no rules, it's

up to you. It's time_____ to come a - live,____ and

D.S. al Coda
(instrumental)

⊕ **Coda**

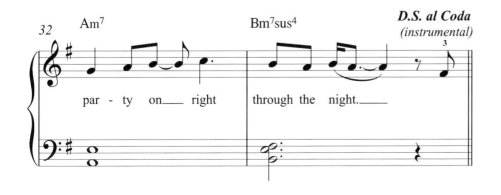

par - ty on___ right through the night.____

One More Chance

Words & Music by R. Kelly

After 'You Are Not Alone' and 'Cry', this was the third song written for Michael Jackson by singer, songwriter and producer R. Kelly and the third time that he recorded a song with this title! The only new track on *Number Ones*, a 2003 greatest hits collection, it was the last original single released during his lifetime.

Hints & Tips: This song has a lot of complicated rhythms, which again will be helped greatly by a supportive, clear accompaniment. It is worth taking time to understand the rhythms properly, especially the semiquaver/dotted quaver rhythms from bar 15 and the rhythm on 'gonna do' in bar 2. It might help with these rhythms to break down each bar into quaver beats in your head or with a metronome before playing the song up to tempo.

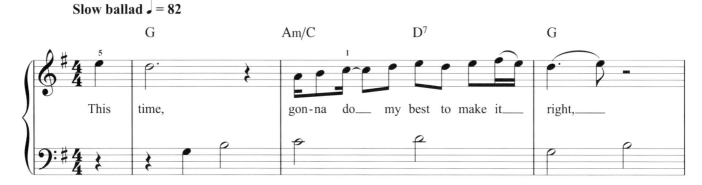

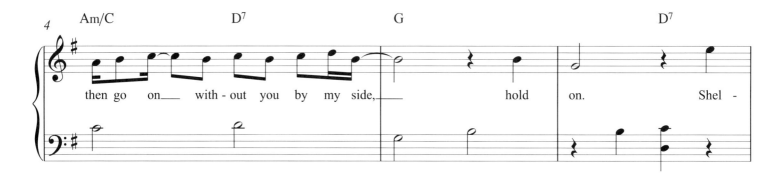

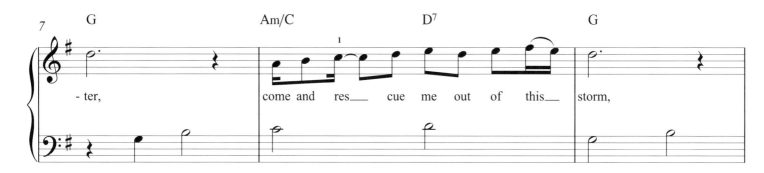

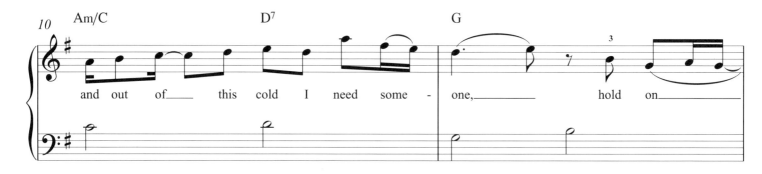

Say Say Say

Words & Music by Michael Jackson & Paul McCartney

In 1982 Michael Jackson and Paul McCartney had collaborated to produce the ballad 'The Girl Is Mine', the first hit single from the album *Thriller*, and Michael returned the favour by duetting on this track for Paul's album *Pipes of Peace*, an even bigger hit which, in 1983, topped the US Billboard Hot 100 for six weeks.

Hints & Tips: Take particular care to employ a heavy, driving accompaniment, being particularly aware of the rests in the left-hand part in bar 2 and other similar places. Try a crescendo from bar 9 to bar 11, as this will fit nicely with the tension in the words.

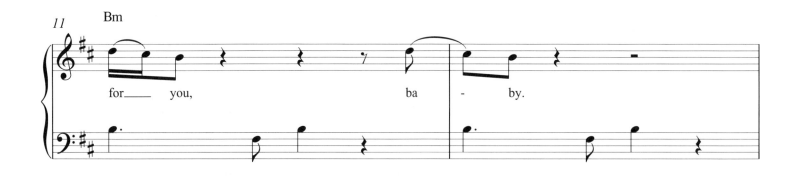

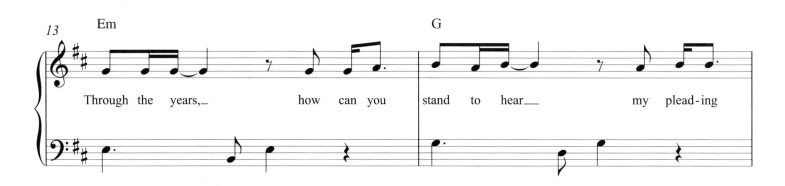

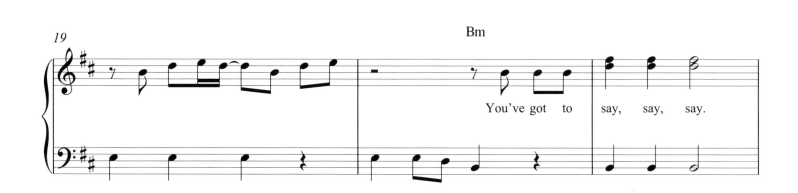

P. Y. T. (Pretty Young Thing)

Words & Music by Quincy Jones & James Ingram

In the guise of 'Pretty Young Things', two of Michael Jackson's sisters, Janet and La Toya, provided backing vocals on this track, the penultimate of seven Top 10 hits from *Thriller*, the top-selling studio album of all time, which in 1984 won a record-breaking eight Grammy Awards and has sold more than 100 million copies worldwide.

Hints & Tips: Notice here the notes on each crotchet beat for most of the first page, this is to make sure that the song has a strong foundation in the accompaniment. Try a small accent on each downbeat. For the the words in brackets (P.Y.T. etc.) you might like to try playing a little quieter. Also experiment with a small ritardando at the end, to make musical sense of the ending.

Rock With You

Words & Music by Rod Temperton

This was the first song Rod Temperton wrote for Michael Jackson and is one of two No. 1 hits from his first solo album as an adult, *Off the Wall*, with which he relaunched his solo career in 1979.

Hints & Tips: This song talks a lot about rhythm, so of course, it is important that it is played with a strong rhythmic sense! Be careful not to rush the triplet at bar 7 and from the second page, the bassline should be strong and driven. From bar 25 the song gradually dies away, so a diminuendo would work nicely.

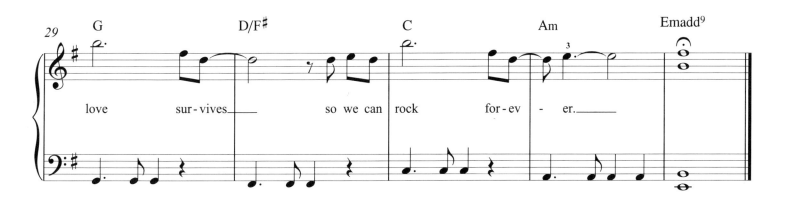

Rockin' Robin

Words & Music by Jimmie Thomas

After having huge success with his brothers in The Jackson 5, the first group in pop history to top the charts with their first four singles, Motown launched Michael Jackson as a solo artist. Jackson's version of this 1958 hit for Bobby Day was included on his debut album *Got To Be There* and in 1972 became his second single.

Hints & Tips: For the first 8 bars the chords on each downbeat should be crisp and energetic. Make sure the chord in bar 3 sounds different from the others by holding it for its full value. From bar 9 the rock rhythm really gets going, so enjoy the strong left-hand rhythm, especially the downbeats.

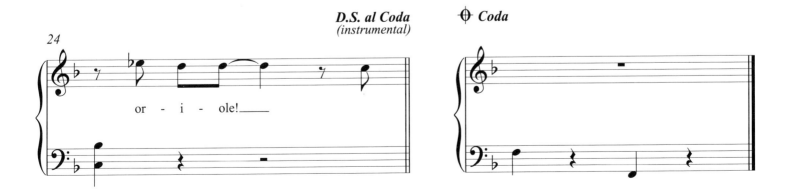

This Is It

Words & Music by Michael Jackson & Paul Anka

Originally written in 1983 this power ballad, featuring backing vocals by Michael's brothers, premiered on his official website in October 2009. It was the first release of new material following his death in June that year, to promote his posthumous album and concert documentary of the same name, although it was only to be aired on radio.

Hints & Tips: Take care of the syncopation that often crosses barlines in this song (like at the first double bar), be sure to hold the notes for their full value as it is easy to cut them too short. Keep the melody flowing and prominant with an even and gentle touch, without letting the accompaniment be too heavy.

You Are Not Alone

Words & Music by R. Kelly

Recorded by Michael Jackson for *HIStory*, his 1995 greatest hits collection, this song became the first single in US history to enter the Billboard charts at No. 1 as well as twice topping the UK charts, the second time in 2009 as recorded by the X-Factor finalists, with all proceeds going to Great Ormond Street Hospital.

Hints & Tips: The accompaniment in this song should be gentle but flowing, taking a short break at bar 5 for the unaccompanied melody line, like the opening. Take time to enjoy the different harmony at bar 23 and try a gradual winding-down towards the end, slightly slowing and with a diminuendo.

Thriller

Words & Music by Rod Temperton

In 1983 Michael Jackson released this rarity, a pop song with a horror theme. The narration and evil laugh at the end were provided by Vincent Price, an actor well known for his work in horror films. Its theatrical 14-minute-long video became one of the most popular ever.

Hints & Tips: We all know the heavy, infectious rhythm of this famous song. Especially in the chorus (from bar 16), each beat should be strong and quite heavy. From bar 25 the rhythm is very important, so take care to work this out and play it in absolute synchronisation with the left hand.

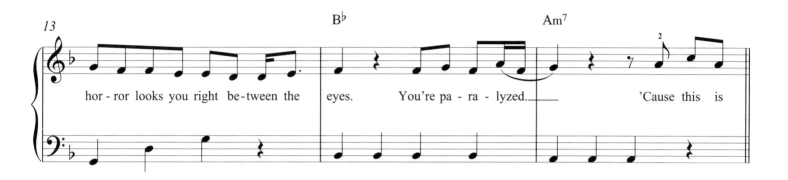

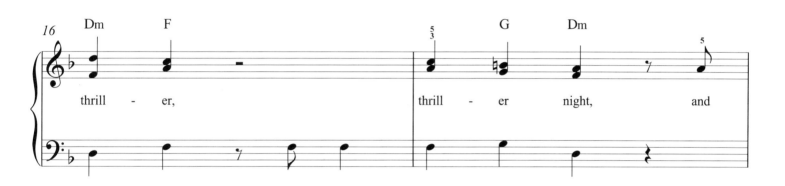

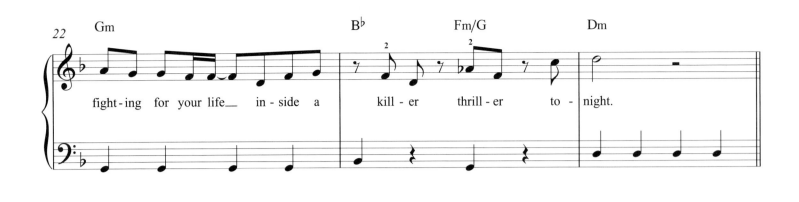

fight-ing for your life__ in-side a killer thrill-er to - night.

Night crea-tures call and the dead start to walk in their

mas - quer - ade. There's no es-cap-in' the

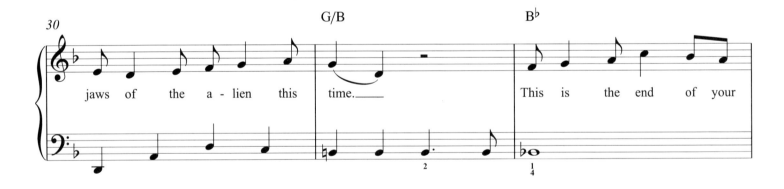

jaws of the a - lien this time.__ This is the end of your

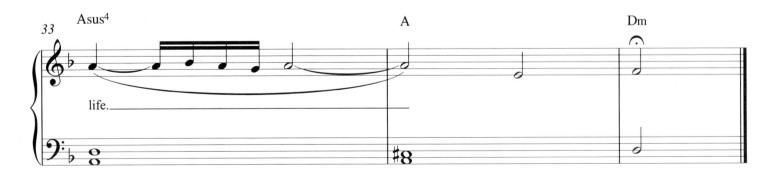

life.__